P9-BJO-037

Cooking Techniques and Recipes with

Olive Oil

Cooking Techniques and Recipes with

Olive Oil

Mary Platis and Laura Bashar

Two Extra Virgins

Cooking Techniques and Recipes with Olive Oil
Copyright © 2014 by Mary Platis and Laura Bashar

All rights reserved. This book was self-published by Mary Platis and Laura Bashar under Two Extra Virgins. No part of this book may be reproduced in any form by any means without the express permission of the authors. This includes reprints, excerpts, photocopying, recording, or any future means of reproducing text.

For more information about permission to reproduce selections from this book, write to: info@twoextravirgins.com

Designed and written by Mary Platis and Laura Bashar
Photography copyright © 2014 by Michael Platis on pages 14, 15, 17, 28, 29, 30.
Cover and all other photography copyright © 2014 by Laura Bashar

Editors: Stephanie Platis and Andrea Susan Glass.

For further information contact:
Two Extra Virgins
www.twoextravirgins.com
Published by Two Extra Virgins
ISBN-10: 0989328929 ISBN-13: 978-0-9893289-2-0

Printed in the United States of America

Because of the risk of food-borne illness, raw or undercooked eggs (and all food and drink recipes that contain them) should not be served to children, the elderly, expectant mothers, or anyone who has immune deficiencies.

Acknowledgements

To my mother Voula Papoulias and my mother-in-law Helen Platis, for encouraging me to cook with fresh ingredients. Thank you for showing me the beauty of the Greek culture, the magical land of Corinth, and the island of Kythira.

～ Mary

To my dearest family for waiting impatiently for dinner to be photographed while your tummies grumbled and for tolerating too many nights during which Mommy/Wife was working on the computer instead of curling up on the couch with all of you.

～ Laura

We would also like to thank John and Bonnie Manion for allowing us to photograph their beautiful garden at Domain de Manion. Thank you to Norman C. Rosen and Stephanie Platis for countlessly reading and editing our cookbook. Thank you to Chef Bridget Bueche for your culinary advice. Thank you to Temecula Olive Oil for letting us roam your olive groves and photograph your beautiful farm. A special thank you to Theodore Panos for believing in our book and supporting us throughout the project. Thank you to Melissa's Produce, Frieda's Produce and Bragg Live Food Products for supplying fabulous ingredients when we needed it. And, thank you to Michael Platis and Reza Bashar for assisting with the editing, recipe sampling, and the endless dish washing.

～ Mary and Laura

Table of Contents

Foreword

I grew up in a large Eastern European family. My grandmother taught all of us from the earliest age that food is the common thread that connects all cultures. We grew much of what we ate, and we canned, preserved, pickled, poached, and stored the rest. Good olive oil was essential in our kitchen.

This lovely primer on one of the basic building blocks of healthy, fresh, delicious food is a gift for anyone wanting to start out on the right foot from the beginning. A successful start makes a journey more enjoyable and impactful. The information, direction, and encouragement contained in this loving homage to an essential component of cookery is to be celebrated as a reference. It is an invitation to buy local, keep it simple, and eat with those you love.

This well written single topic book offers an opportunity to expand one's specific knowledge base of olive oil, its origins, and the regional flavors. It also gives the reader an opportunity to learn specific cooking techniques such

as marinating, braising, poaching, and even baking with this lovely and versatile ingredient. Get ready to broaden your experience of cooking with olive oil from simple salad dressings to braised lamb shanks with rosemary, garlic, and gigante beans.

Enjoy this delicious road map on your journey to incorporate healthy, delicious olive oil into your culinary repertoire.

I'm off to the store for some fresh ingredients and good local olive oil! Opa!

~ Candy Wallace

Chef, Author, Culinary Educator, Speaker

Founder and Executive Director of
American Personal & Private Chef Association

*I*n the fall of 2001, Nancy Curry and I started a small production olive oil company. Our dream was to produce a high quality extra virgin olive oil and share the delicious taste of our fresh handcrafted olive oil. We simply started sharing our discovery with anyone that would listen.

Our commitment to give our families and friends the best we can produce is a joy that is reinforced daily. It is encouraging to find how many people love to share their recipes and stories of family and friends gathering at the table. We have found that an abundance in the garden turns into an opportunity to share. We share our extra vegetables, fruits and harvests of all kinds and savor the numerous recipe ideas that come in return. Finding simple recipes for simple high quality ingredients makes it easy to live a healthy life.

We know you will enjoy the truly wonderful recipes in this book and will explore the never ending possibilities of using fresh olive oil. As we have always stated, "Everything we do should be centered around family, food and fun."

Enjoy!

~ Catherine Pepe, Nancy and Thom Curry

Temecula Olive Oil Company

"May olive your dreams come true"

Introduction

How often do you come home from buying a beautiful bottle of extra virgin olive oil and wish you had more uses for it other than a salad dressing or sautéing up a quick dish? In this book you will learn the easy cooking techniques of poaching, braising, marinating, infusing, and baking with olive oil. Our goal is to teach you a new way of cooking and to help you master fundamental skills.

The cooking techniques in this book will sharpen your skills in the kitchen and acquaint cooks at all levels with these basic methods. Don't expect it to be overnight. Learning proper cooking techniques will take time, patience, practice, and repetition. Soon, developing your own recipes will become easy and effortless, and you will have the knowledge and skills you need to successfully use olive oil in all your meals.

We chose Mediterranean recipes because most olive oils come from that region. But if you are fortunate to live in a state that produces local olive oil, we encourage you to buy locally and meet your farmers. We kept these recipes simple so you can have fun in the kitchen!

*M*eet Mary Platis

In a Greek household, olive oil serves many purposes. Not only is it a staple in the kitchen, it's a key ingredient in every aspect of our lives. As a young girl, I remember watching my mother slather her arms and hands with olive oil. She would combine avocado, eggs, and olive oil into a lotion and spread it over her face as a weekend cleansing mask. Now, I watch my husband use olive oil to remove motor oil and dirt from his hands after a long day in the garage. Who would have guessed? I often ask myself, "What don't Greeks use olive oil for?"

Though olive oil was always an integral part of my life, a recent trip to Greece changed the way I now think about it. My husband and I spent several days on Kythera, the island from which my husband's family immigrated. We toured ancient olive groves and experienced the entire process of making olive oil from olive to oil. I developed a newfound respect for first press and organic extra virgin olive oil due to the extensive hours of hard work that are required to produce a single bottle.

As a chef, I try to incorporate extra virgin olive oil into my cooking classes, blog recipes, and home-cooked meals in any way imaginable. The more I learn about the endless uses of extra virgin olive oil, the more confidence I gain in cooking with this truly extraordinary ingredient. I continue to share these lessons through my recipes and cooking techniques on my food blog California Greek Girl – and now, you, too, can master the use of olive oil.

Meet Laura Bashar

From my earliest memory, food has always been the center of family gatherings. Whether we were watching my grandmother carefully fan the flames for the perfect kabob or gathering with cousins to compare notes on our favorite dishes, we always talked about food or talked in the presence of food. My mother is Iranian, my father American. I was raised eating gourmet meals ranging from Persian stews to shrimp scampi. Growing up, my mom loved to cook despite working full time as a micro-paleontologist.

I often helped start family dinners, and I loved trying to create eccentric dishes that I read about in cookbooks. Even when I was a young advertising executive, long before food blogs made their appearance, I collected magazines, tested the recipes I saw, and continued my journey with food.

And now, with a family of my own, I am teaching the same culinary lessons to my children. Their palate is refined. They recognize quality ingredients. To put it bluntly, they are spoiled. And why not? Why should bland starchy foods be the norm on the American dinner plate?

The first time I recognized quality in something as simple as olive oil was at an Italian restaurant, where I was served exquisite olive oil in which to bathe my freshly baked bread. I was in heaven. This was not the same olive oil I found at the supermarket. I closed my eyes and let the flavors take me to far and exotic places. I still have not opened my eyes.

My cooking philosophy is to choose high quality, wholesome ingredients and let them shine and take center stage. It's about the food, the family gathered before it, and the love that is shared around the table. I share this love on my blog Family Spice.

Chapter 1
A Lesson on Olive Oil

Olive Oil History

The olive tree is one of the oldest known cultivated trees in the world. In fact, fossilized olive leaves 37,000 years old have been discovered on the Greek island of Santorini. Olive trees quickly spread to the rest of the Mediterranean basin, where the ancient Greeks, Egyptians, and Romans used olives and its oil as a fixture in their daily lives. As a result, over the centuries we have had countless varieties of olives to choose from. Although Spain produces most of the world's olive oil, you can also find varieties from Greece, Italy, France, Australia, California, and many other places around the world. However, the Greeks are the largest per capita consumers of olive oil worldwide.

California history is not only famous for its Gold Rush, but also a booming olive oil industry that started in San Diego. In 1769, Franciscan fathers from Mexico introduced the olive and began planting olive tree groves in their fields in Southern California. It was Juniper Sierra who built the first Mission San Diego de Acala and brought with him olive tree cuttings of what we

identify today as the Mission olive. Historical writings document that olive oil production was in full swing in the early 1800s amongst the many California missions. Cuttings from the first Mission olive tree would supply new missions with olives as they were built along the California coastline. Olive groves flourished in the perfect climate and conditions found in the Southwest.

Olive demand boomed, with the table olive dominating most of the 20th century. Unable to compete with the prices of imported olives, California turned to producing its own olive oil. With over 47,000 acres of olive trees in California today (27,000 acres for olives, 20,000 for oil), California has become the third largest producer of olive oil worldwide.

Today, California is producing award-winning olive oils. U.S. production has reached 1.5 million liters (396,000 gallons) and Americans consume over 210 million liters (5.5 million gallons) of olive oil annually.

Olive Oil Production

oday, olive oil is produced all over the world from small family farms to large corporate growers. New olive oil making technology, along with advanced research on olive farming, has enabled producers to make the best olive oil ever made.

To meet the legal requirements for taste and chemical properties of the extra virgin grade, oil must be made from healthy, expertly picked olives and milled within 24 hours of harvest to preserve their flavor and avoid spoilage.

Olive harvesting can occur at various stages of the olive's development. Green immature fruits are the earliest to be picked. Veraison, the green to yellow fruit, is picked next, while the last is the black (mature) fruit when the olive turns from purple to black. Each of these olives produce different flavors.

The actual production process today is similar to what has been done for thousands of years. Although some farmers do embrace new technology while others use traditional methods.

The olives can be picked several ways: by hand, with handheld devices, with air-powered combs, or with a shaker harvester. The olives are placed in bins with water to remove leaves and stems. Olives are then sent to large stainless steel tanks where they are washed.

Once washed, they are sent to the mill where the olives, pits, and flesh are ground to form a paste. The paste is then piped onto wire mesh disks where they are stacked to squeeze out the oil. The liquid is then transferred into stainless steel containers allowing the sediment to sink down, or the oil is passed through a sieve-like screen to filter out the sediment. The water and oil naturally separate and the oil is then bottled and stored.

Again, a good olive oil is produced when the farmer takes the time to pick, press, and bottle with high standards and the proper techniques.

Olive Oil Varieties

*T*he flavor of olive oil can change dramatically depending on the climate, soil conditions, and the processing of the olives resulting in the numerous varieties we have today. There are over 700 olive cultivars in the world, each of which produces one-of-a-kind flavor profiles with unique nutritional and chemical properties. The picture above shows a collection of various olive oils from around the world. Color is not an indicator of quality.

As you cook and use olive oil daily, you will become more familiar with the many different varieties and their characteristics. Take a trip to a local olive grove, farmer's market or olive oil specialty store for a tasting so you can determine which olive oil suits your taste.

Once you begin to taste different varieties of olive oil, you will begin to notice slight to extreme differences in the flavors and bite. Think of olive oil as you would wine. What determines these taste variations are the type of olives, climate, and how early or late in the harvest season they were pressed. Harvest begins in October and ends in February.

The olive changes color and flavor the longer it stays on the tree and begins to ripen. It starts out green, it moves to green-yellow, then changes to red, then purple, until it is (finally) very black. When the olives are harvested early in the season, in October, a greener more robust oil is

produced. The taste is a more leafy green and leaves a burning sensation in the throat, but it has more healthful properties. Olives harvested in late January through February will be black and produce a milder oil.

Fragrant and fruity olive oil is typically from Spanish olives that are almost but not fully ripe. A greener and peppery taste comes from Tuscan-style varieties. Leafy-green, grassy flavors develop mostly from Spanish and Greek olives pressed earlier in the year, which makes them strong and peppery. Whichever you decide on purchasing, enjoy olive oil liberally.

Listed below are just a few of the hundred different varieties of olives produced in the European and California regions:
• Greece: Koroneiki, Lianolia, Chrondrolia, Adramytini
• Spain: Picual, Arbequina, Hojiblanca, Manzanillo
• Italy: Frantoio, Leccnio, Pendolino, Moraiolo
• France: Picholine, Lucques, Bouteillan, Grossane
• California: Mission, Manzanillo, Arbosana, Arbequina
• Australia: Frantoio, Correggiola, Pendulina, Barouni

Olive oils flavored with fruits or herbs are also available. These oils are either made with heat infusion, explained in Chapter 7, or the fruits or herbs are pressed with the olives during the production process. Flavored olive oils offer another dimension to your cooking.

*O*ne liter of olive oil is produced from the pressing of seven liters of olives.

Selecting and Storing Olive Oil

*P*urchasing olive oil should be a simple and enjoyable experience. For the best quality, you should only consider buying extra virgin olive oil. Labels stating light, extra light, pure, virgin or just plain olive oil are not 100% extra virgin olive oil. These oils have been proven to have been altered by chemicals, diluted with other oils or were not produced according to industry standards for extra virgin olive oil.

An easy definition for extra virgin olive oil to remember is that it belongs in the category of "Freshly Squeezed Fruit Juice," whereas everything else is of lesser quality. Check the label for ingredients when shopping. If the word "refined oil" is listed, this means that it has been chemically produced and is not extra virgin olive oil.

Olive oil contains a high monounsaturated fat content, which allows it to be stored longer than other oils. Store olive oil in a dark cool place in your

kitchen, away from the stove or other heating elements to prolong its shelf life. Most experts recommend you store olive oil at room temperature, especially high-quality extra virgin olive oil. Olive oil kept in a dark environment can last up to one year opened, and up to two years if left unopened. Replace the bottle if it is not dark and store the oil in a stainless steel container or a dark bottle.

Here are some quick tips:
• Shop at a store you can trust that has hand-selected, fine quality olive oils.
• Buy olive oil with a harvest date stamp on the label to ensure freshness.
• Buy a small quantity, so you use up the oil within one year.
• Buy olive oil in a dark bottle for protection against sunlight.
• Do not choose an oil by its color. Instead, you should smell and taste it.

$\mathcal{O}$live oil stored in clear bottles left exposed to light, whether sunlight or artificial, will turn rancid.

Cooking with Olive Oil

*O*live oil is a staple of the Mediterranean diet – and largely responsible for making it one of the healthiest and delectable diets in the world. Like a fine wine or exquisite cut of meat, olive oil is known for its dynamic and diverse flavor characteristics. Understanding basic olive oil profiles will hopefully inspire you to experiment with new flavor combinations in your dishes and encourage you to cook ethnic foods with oils from different regions.

Olive oils have varying characteristics and can be identified by using descriptive phrases similar to wines:

Robust flavor: Pungent, spicy, peppery (felt in the throat). Use strong and robust extra virgin olive oils for your meats to make marinades or to drizzle on peppers or garlic.

Medium flavor: Fruity, olive, green (grassy, leaves, apples, other fruit). Use a well-rounded extra virgin olive oil for breads, baking, steamed vegetables, and dips.

Delicate flavor: Mild, buttery, sweet taste. This oil can be incorporated in cakes, cookies, and sauces.

Flavored olive oils are a wonderful way to enhance the flavor in your foods. Fruit flavored olive oils, like citrus, can be used in salad dressings, cakes, cookies, and drinks. Choose an herb flavored olive oil for more savory creations like breads, vegetables, and soups. Most importantly, do not be afraid to experiment. For example, a basil or mint flavored olive oil would be a terrific addition to a cocktail.

*T*he key to cooking with olive oil is your personal palate. If you do not like the flavor of the olive oil, do not use it in your cooking!

The Mediterranean Diet

When people ask what the Mediterranean diet is, you must think "olive oil." Along the Mediterranean Sea runs a long tradition of growing, producing, harvesting, and cooking with olive oil. As a result, the Mediterranean diet is becoming more and more popular as people seek healthy ways of eating and living.

One important element of this diet, which most people are not familiar with, is the lifestyle. The Mediterranean diet is not just about what you eat, it's about how you eat. In other words, it's a way of life. Mediterranean families almost always prep, cook, and eat dinner together. A glass of red wine is often the drink of choice with meals, but many people also drink tea. Staying active – from taking long walks to gardening or attending community events – is another critical aspect of this culture. Having a belief system based in religion or like minds to keep the mind and body healthy is also highly valued in the Mediterranean lifestyle. When all of these factors are combined with great food, it's no wonder that health and longevity are improved.

Many people have adopted the Mediterranean diet in the U.S. because it is a plant-based diet, which means that it supports eating less meat and consuming more wild greens, grains, beans, vegetables, nuts, and fruits. The Harvard School of Public Health developed a food pyramid that is based on this diet by conducting a study of the inhabitants of Ikaria, Greece, and the Sicilians of southern Italy. They and many other researchers, such as Blue Zone Research, have found that the longest living centenarians (people who live to 100 and above) lived in these regions. One important key to a healthy diet is to substitute good fats for bad fats and to avoid trans-fats.

This returns us to the subject of olive oil. The love of olive oil is the common thread that the Mediterranean culture embraces in their everyday life. Extra virgin olive oil is the only oil they use in their daily cooking. Everyday researchers are discovering more remarkable health benefits from consuming extra virgin olive oil.

Chapter 2
Poaching with Olive Oil

Poaching with Olive Oil

Poaching in olive oil is a technique that transfers heat from the olive oil to the item being cooked. Always poach at a gentle simmer around 160-180°F. The meat that is being poached should be totally submerged in the olive oil. An instant-read thermometer is necessary for an accurate gauge of readiness. When you think about the meat being cooked, think of it as being in a nice warm bath. Vegetables can be partially submerged and the same results are achieved.

So why poach meats or vegetables in a bath of olive oil when there are a multitude of other methods? Just try it and you will become a convert. The meat or vegetable emerges evenly cooked and immensely tender with a subtle hint of the oil's flavors. Adding herbs and spices to the oil further elevates the aromatic qualities and taste of a dish.

Tips on Poaching:

• Find the right size pot, not too big, not too small. Food should be snug but not touching.
• A "quivering" movement is the right description of the liquid temperature.
• The poaching oil can be reused again, whether for a vinaigrette or in cooking.
• To reuse the oil, bring the poaching liquid to a low boil, then allow to cool. Strain the oil and discard bits. Oil can be refrigerated for up to one week.

$\mathcal{R}$osemary-Garlic Lamb Chops with Mashed Potatoes and Artichokes

$\mathcal{T}$una with Citrus and Avocado Salad

$\mathcal{C}$hicken Breasts with Asparagus and Pea Orzo

$\mathcal{T}$omatoes and Onions in Olive Oil with Fresh Basil

$\mathcal{S}$hrimp with Sweet Potato Pecan Mash

$\mathcal{F}$igs with Muscato Grapes

Thick lamb loin chops are poached in a fragrant garlic and rosemary bath. Add these lovely silken potatoes as a standout side dish and you have a true Mediterranean meal.

Rosemary-Garlic Lamb Chops with Mashed Potatoes and Artichokes

SERVES 4
PREP TIME: 15 MINUTES
COOK TIME: 30 MINUTES

LAMB CHOPS

8 lamb loin chops (about 1-inch thick)
1 teaspoon salt
½ teaspoon freshly ground pepper
2-4 cups extra virgin olive oil
2 garlic cloves, crushed
2 sprigs fresh rosemary

GARNISH

½ teaspoon sea salt
1 tomato, chopped
¼ cup canned artichoke hearts, in water, drained and chopped
1 green onion, chopped

MASHED POTATOES

4 russet potatoes, peeled and coarsely chopped
4 garlic cloves, peeled
½ cup warm milk
¼ cup extra virgin olive oil
One 13.75-ounce can artichoke hearts in water, drained, chopped
½ teaspoon salt
¼ teaspoon freshly ground pepper

1. Preheat oven to 225ºF. Choose an ovenproof baking dish or pan large enough to submerge the chops without touching one another.

2. Add rosemary and garlic to the pan and sprinkle chops with salt and pepper on both sides. Add chops to the pan.

3. Pour olive oil into the pan, covering all chops completely, and place pan in the oven.

4. After 20 minutes turn chops over in the oil, and return pan to the oven for another 10 minutes.

5. Using an instant-read thermometer, cook until desired doneness. Temperature for medium is 160ºF.

6. While lamb chops are cooking, place a large pot of salted water on high heat and bring to a boil.

7. Add chopped potatoes and garlic. Bring back to a boil and reduce heat to medium. Cook 15 to 20 minutes until a knife inserted into potatoes removes easily. Drain potatoes.

8. Place potatoes back in warm pan to remove any excess moisture. Mash potatoes using a ricer, food mill, or mash by hand with a fork or spoon.

9. Add warm milk and olive oil. Stir until thoroughly mixed. Stir chopped artichokes into potatoes and mix thoroughly. Add salt and pepper.

10. Remove lamb chops, lift them out of the oil, and place on a paper towel to drain.

11. Before serving, sprinkle with sea salt, tomato, artichoke, and onion for garnish.

Deliciously moist tuna steaks are elegantly cooked in an orange-scented olive oil bath and served with a butter lettuce salad and a trio of citrus fruits.

Tuna with Citrus and Avocado Salad

SERVES 4
PREP TIME: 25 MINUTES
COOK TIME: 20 MINUTES

TUNA

Four 1-inch thick tuna steaks
½ teaspoon salt
¼ teaspoon freshly ground pepper
2-4 cups extra virgin olive oil
zest from 1 orange
2 bay leaves

SALAD

1 large head of butter lettuce
2 avocados, peeled and sliced
1 orange, peeled and segmented
1 grapefruit, peeled and segmented
1 tangerine, peeled and segmented
½ red onion, peeled and sliced
½ cup sliced almonds, toasted

VINAIGRETTE

¼ cup rice wine vinegar
½ teaspoon salt
½ cup extra virgin olive oil
½ cup fresh cilantro, chopped
¼ teaspoon freshly ground pepper

1. Preheat oven to 225ºF. Choose an ovenproof baking dish or pan large enough to submerge tuna steaks without touching one another.

2. Sprinkle both sides of tuna steaks with salt and pepper.

3. Pour cold oil into the pan and place in oven until oil temperature reaches 180ºF.

4. Add orange zest and bay leaves to the oil. Slowly drop in tuna steaks.

5. Return pan to the oven and cook for 20 minutes. Tuna must be cooked thoroughly and have an internal temperature of 130ºF. Because the tuna is being heated at such a low temperature, only when it is completely cooked can you insure that any bacteria has been removed.

6. Place tuna steaks on a plate and keep warm.

7. While the tuna rests, prepare the salad. Tear lettuce into bite size pieces, divide evenly, and place onto four plates.

8. Add avocados, orange, grapefruit, tangerine, and onion. Sprinkle almonds on top.

9. For the vinaigrette, add vinegar and salt in a small bowl. Whisk to blend. Slowly add olive oil and continue whisking until blended. Add cilantro and pepper and whisk thoroughly.

10. Place tuna steaks on the plate along with salad. Add the vinaigrette.

The flavors in this poached chicken will whisk you off to an alfresco dinner in the Greek countryside. The orzo and farm fresh vegetables complete the flavors of the Aegean Sea.

Chicken Breasts with Asparagus and Pea Orzo

SERVES 4
PREP TIME: 15 MINUTES
COOK TIME: 30 MINUTES

CHICKEN

4 chicken breasts, boneless and skinless
1 teaspoon salt
½ teaspoon freshly ground pepper
2 leeks, washed and cut into rounds
    (white only)
2 sprigs fresh oregano
2-4 cups extra virgin olive oil

GARNISH

1 fresh tomato, chopped
¼ cup parsley, chopped
¼ teaspoon salt
⅛ teaspoon freshly ground pepper

ORZO

4 quarts water
1 teaspoon salt
2 cups uncooked orzo
1 bunch asparagus, trimmed and
    chopped into 1-inch pieces
4-5 teaspoons olive oil, divided
2 cups frozen peas, defrosted
4 green onions, chopped
½ cup toasted pine nuts
½ cup freshly grated parmesan cheese
juice from ½ lemon

1. Preheat oven to 225°F. Choose an ovenproof baking dish or pan large enough to submerge chicken breasts without touching one another.

2. Add leeks and oregano in the bottom of the pan. Sprinkle breasts with salt and pepper on both sides. Add chicken to the pan.

3. Pour olive oil in the pan enough to cover chicken.

4. Place the pan in the oven and cook for 20 minutes. Turn chicken and cook for another 10 minutes.

5. Check chicken with a meat thermometer and remove when temperature reaches 165°F.

6. While chicken is cooking, bring a large pot of water to boil and add salt. Slowly add orzo, stir, and return to a boil. Continue cooking for 5 minutes.

7. Add asparagus pieces to the orzo and continue cooking for an additional 3 minutes or until asparagus is fork tender. Drain and transfer to a large bowl. Stir in 2 to 3 teaspoons of olive oil.

8. Add peas, green onions, and pine nuts to the orzo and mix gently. Stir in parmesan cheese and add remaining oil and lemon.

9. Combine garnish ingredients in a small bowl.

10. When chicken is done, place each breast on a plate and top with garnish. Serve with orzo.

There is nothing like the taste of warm tomatoes poached with two classic flavors, spicy garlic and sweet fresh basil. Serve the tomatoes straight from the dish, rustic-style, with slices of freshly baked bread.

Tomatoes and Onions in Olive Oil with Fresh Basil

SERVES 4
PREP TIME: 10 MINUTES
COOK TIME: 45 TO 60 MINUTES

3 large tomatoes, peeled and cored
3 large onions, peeled and cored
12 fresh basil leaves
3-4 cups extra virgin olive oil
6 garlic cloves, peeled
½ teaspoon salt
¼ teaspoon freshly ground pepper
2-3 fresh basil leaves, julienned for garnish
1 loaf artisan bread, sliced and toasted

1. Heat oven to 375ºF. Line the bottom of a large ovenproof dish with basil leaves.

2. Place tomatoes and onions core side down in the dish so they are snug but not touching.

3. Pour enough olive oil to cover tomatoes and onions halfway up its sides. Add and submerge garlic cloves in the oil.

4. Bake for 45 to 60 minutes or until tomatoes and onions are soft.

5. Sprinkle with salt, pepper, and freshly sliced basil.

6. Slice and toast the bread and serve with the warm tomatoes and onions. Poaching liquid can also be served.

*T*ry using other vegetables like eggplant, leeks, artichokes, and fennel.

Use a flavorful extra virgin olive oil to poach the shrimp. Prepare the sweet potatoes and have them warm and ready to serve as the shrimp is removed from the oil. One final squeeze of lime juice will bring the two dishes together.

Shrimp with Sweet Potato Pecan Mash

SERVES 4
PREP TIME: 15 MINUTES
COOK TIME: 30 MINUTES

SWEET POTATO MASH

2 large sweet potatoes, peeled and cut
  into 1-inch rounds
2 tablespoons extra virgin olive oil
4 tablespoons maple syrup
2 teaspoons brown sugar
zest of 1 lime
½ teaspoon cinnamon
½ cup toasted pecans, chopped

SHRIMP

16 jumbo shrimp, cleaned and deveined
2-3 cups extra virgin olive oil
One 3-inch long cinnamon stick
juice and peel from 1 lime
2 dried red chilies
1 teaspoon salt
½ teaspoon freshly ground pepper

1. Place sweet potato rounds in a medium pot and cover with water. Bring to boil and cook until potatoes are fork tender, about 15 to 20 minutes.

2. Drain potatoes and return them to the pot. Add olive oil and mash until smooth.

3. Stir in maple syrup, brown sugar, zest and cinnamon. Cover potatoes and keep warm.

4. Wash and clean the shrimp. Pat dry with paper towels.

5. Sprinkle both sides of shrimp with salt and pepper.

6. Pour olive oil into a wide deep saucepan. Add cinnamon stick, lime peel, and dried chilies.

7. Carefully add in shrimp.

8. Cook on stove until temperature reaches 180ºF, and simmer for 10 minutes until shrimp are pink and cooked.

9. Remove and drain shrimp on paper towels.

10. To serve, divide the shrimp onto 4 plates and drizzle with lime juice. Add a serving of sweet potatoes and garnish with chopped pecans.

This is a unique dish you can present as an elegant appetizer or a simple dessert. Serve with fresh bread and goat cheese to make crostinis. Choose a spicy olive oil for more flavor. Small green figs hold their shape the best.

Figs with Muscato Grapes

SERVES 8-10
PREP TIME: 10 MINUTES
COOK TIME: 20 MINUTES

16 medium size green figs, about 1½ pints
2 large bunches of Muscato grapes or
    any dark purple grape
2 dried star anise
2 sprigs of fresh rosemary
3 fresh basil leaves
2 pinches of red pepper flakes
2 garlic cloves, peeled
¼ teaspoon vanilla extract
¾-1 cup extra virgin olive oil

1. Preheat oven to 350ºF. Place figs in a single layer into an 8x8 pan or larger.

2. Remove grapes from the stems and add to the pan, placing them snugly between the figs.

3. Add anise, rosemary, basil, red pepper flakes, garlic, and vanilla to the pan.

4. Pour enough olive oil to cover figs halfway up its sides.

5. Bake in oven for 15 to 20 minutes or until figs and grapes are tender.

6. Remove and let cool to room temperature.

7. Serve one fig with several grapes in individual bowls or cups. Drizzle 1 teaspoon of poaching liquid on top.

8. Can be made the day ahead and refrigerated.

Other uses:
• Serve warm over vanilla ice cream
• Serve with soft goat cheese as a crostini
• Use as a topping for fish or chicken
• Add to a warm spinach salad
• Mix in a warm quinoa or bulgar salad

Chapter 3
Braising with Olive Oil

Braising with Olive Oil

Braising is a gentle, slow cooking technique in which the food is browned first, then finished by simmering. Of all the techniques in the book, this one will bring you the best results if you keep a few key steps in mind. Most braises involve larger cuts of meat and less liquid than stews. But the key here is to keep the temperature low, well below boiling, at 180°F. The cooked meat should be allowed to cool in the liquid, and is best served below the cooking temperature. Most braises taste better the next day, once the flavors have had time to develop.

Best Cuts for Braising:
Beef: Chuck, Blade Roast, Brisket, Short Ribs, Bottom Round
Lamb: Shoulder and Shanks
Pork: Shoulder and Spare Ribs
Poultry: Whole Bird, Thighs and Legs
Fish: Tuna, Salmon, Halibut, Bass, Red Snapper

Tips on Braising:

• Keep the meat in large pieces no smaller than 2 inches to preserve the juices.

• Brown, or sear, the meat very quickly in a hot pan to prevent cooking the inside of the meat.

• Do not cover the meat with liquid, as adding too much liquid will dilute the flavors of the dish.

• Cook for long periods of time, and stop cooking when the meat is easily pierced by a fork. Remove the meat from the pan before making a sauce with the leftover liquid.

• A heavy-gauge pot with a lid is ideal because it distributes the heat evenly and helps to protect the foods from cooking too quickly.

Fresh Tomato Risotto

Chicken with Carrots and Fennel

Lamb Shanks with Rosemary, Garlic, and Gigante Beans

Greek Style Vegetables with Tomatoes

Beef Stew with Root Vegetables

What could be better than fresh tomatoes with risotto? This is a match made in heaven: warm creamy Arborio rice steeped in a tomato sauce with freshly picked basil. Perfect for a quick hearty lunch or a casual summer supper on the porch. Bellissimo!

Fresh Tomato Risotto

SERVES 4
PREP TIME: 15 MINUTES
COOK TIME: 30 MINUTES

RISOTTO

4 cups chicken or vegetable stock
6 tomatoes, seeded and coarsely
   chopped
4-6 fresh basil leaves
4 teaspoons extra virgin olive oil, divided
3 garlic cloves, finely chopped
2 cups Arborio rice
2 teaspoons dried oregano
1-2 teaspoons salt
½ teaspoon freshly ground pepper
2 teaspoons butter
½ cup freshly grated parmesan cheese

GARNISH

1-2 fresh tomatoes, sliced
3-4 basil leaves, julienned

1. Bring the stock to a simmer over low heat in a medium size pot.

2. In a small saucepan, add tomatoes and basil and cook on low until warm. Remove basil.

3. Place a large Dutch oven or a deep 4-quart skillet over medium heat. Add 2 teaspoons olive oil. When the olive oil is sizzling, add garlic and stir for 2 minutes.

4. Stir rice and oregano into the pot and braise for 2 more minutes.

5. Begin adding the warm tomatoes slowly into the rice, 1 cup at a time, stirring continuously. Cook until all liquid has been absorbed and continue stirring. Add remainder of tomatoes in batches until all the sauce has been used.

6. Season with salt and pepper.

7. Stir in the stock, 1 cup at a time, until all of it has been added.

8. Taste again and adjust the seasonings. It is perfectly cooked when the rice is tender to the bite, approximately 30 to 40 minutes.

9. Stir in butter and parmesan cheese. Drizzle with remaining 2 teaspoons of olive oil.

10. Garnish with a slice of fresh tomato on each plate and sprinkle with basil.

If you are craving comfort food, turn to this classic Greek chicken dish where thighs and legs are braised in wine and lemon juice, then slow-cooked with warm fall vegetables. Serve alone or with a grain like rice or green salad.

Chicken with Carrots and Fennel

SERVES 4
PREP TIME: 15 MINUTES
COOK TIME: 30 MINUTES

CHICKEN

4 chicken drumsticks
4 chicken thighs
1 teaspoon salt
½ teaspoon freshly ground pepper
2 teaspoons extra virgin olive oil
2 fennel bulbs, topped, cored, and sliced
2 pounds carrots, peeled, quartered, and sliced lengthwise
½ cup freshly squeezed lemon juice
½ cup white wine
½ cup chicken broth

GARNISH

½ cup olives, pitted
1 tablespoon capers, rinsed
½ cup chopped fresh parsley, chopped

1. Wash and pat dry chicken. Salt and pepper both sides.

2. Add olive oil to a large Dutch oven, and cook over medium heat.

3. When oil is hot, add chicken and brown on both sides, about 5 minutes for each side. Remove chicken from the pan and place on a plate.

4. Add fennel and carrots to the pot and braise for 4 to 5 minutes until slightly cooked.

5. Return chicken to the pot with vegetables, adding lemon juice and wine.

6. Bring to a boil, then reduce to a simmer. Cook until juices from chicken run clear, about 45 minutes to 1 hour.

7. If needed, add chicken broth to prevent any scorching.

8. Remove from the pan and serve with garnish.

*T*ry braising other seasonal vegetables like artichokes, potatoes, and mushrooms.

This traditional lamb dish is braised with garlic and rosemary for 3 hours, so plan ahead and enjoy the lovely aroma permeating your house as the dish slowly cooks.

Lamb Shanks with Rosemary, Garlic, and Gigante Beans

SERVES 6
PREP TIME: 10 MINUTES
COOK TIME: 4 HOURS

LAMB

6 lamb shanks (1 to 1½ pounds each)
1 teaspoon salt
½ teaspoon freshly ground pepper
6 carrots, peeled and sliced lengthwise
Two 6-inch sprigs of fresh rosemary

BRAISING SAUCE

2 cups red wine
1 cup extra virgin olive oil
½ cup fresh lemon juice
¼ cup fresh garlic, chopped
½ teaspoon salt
½ teaspoon freshly ground pepper

GIGANTE BEANS

2 cups dried gigante beans, soaked over
    night or 16-ounce can large lima beans
4 teaspoons extra virgin olive oil, divided
1 celery stalk, chopped
1 carrot, chopped
½ small onion, chopped
2 garlic cloves, finely chopped
2 tomatoes, seeded and coarsely
    chopped
1 cup broth (chicken or vegetable)
½ cup parsley, finely chopped
1 teaspoon salt
½ teaspoon freshly ground pepper
1 teaspoon dried oregano

1. Preheat oven to 400°F.

2. Season shanks with salt and pepper. Place shanks on a hot grill or sauté pan and brown on all sides, about 15 minutes.

3. Whisk together ingredients for braising sauce.

4. Transfer shanks to a deep ovenproof casserole dish and pour sauce over them. Be certain to completely cover lamb with the liquid. Place sprigs of rosemary around the shanks. If not enough sauce is covering them, add additional wine or some broth.

5. Cover the dish tightly with foil and place in the middle of a hot oven. Roast for 3 hours.

6. Remove from oven and add carrots. Cover again and cook for 1 more hour. The lamb is done when the meat is easily pierced with a fork and is falling off the bone.

7. Heat a deep sauté pan over medium heat and add 2 teaspoons of olive oil.

8. Stir in celery, carrot, onion, garlic, tomatoes, and broth. If using canned lima beans, add during last 10 minutes of cooking. If using soaked gigante beans, drain beans and add to vegetables. Cook for 15 minutes.

9. Stir in parsley, salt, pepper, and oregano.

10. Reduce heat to simmer, cover pan, and cook for 45 minutes. Again, if using canned lima beans, add beans during last 10 minutes of cooking.

11. When shanks are done, remove from oven and allow them to rest for 10 minutes.

12. Transfer lamb to a serving dish and top with beans. Drizzle with remaining 2 teaspoons of olive oil and oregano.

This dish is commonly found in Greek households and is often made with what is available from the garden that day. Braising vegetables allows the flavors to blend together for a delicious meal. It is normally served with a nice chunk of bread and tastes even better the next day!

Greek Style Vegetables with Tomatoes

SERVES 6
PREP TIME: 20 MINUTES
COOK TIME: 1 HOUR

4 teaspoons extra virgin olive oil, divided
1 onion, peeled and sliced
3 garlic cloves, chopped
3 russet potatoes, peeled, sliced in half, and quartered lengthwise
4 carrots, peeled and sliced in half
½ pound green beans, trimmed
4 zucchini, halved lengthwise and cut into 2-inch pieces
1 large eggplant, chopped into 1-inch pieces
2 tomatoes, chopped or 4 ounces tomato sauce
2 teaspoons dried oregano
½ teaspoon salt
¼ teaspoon freshly ground pepper
2 teaspoons fresh parsley, chopped

1. Preheat oven to 350ºF.

2. Place a large sauté pan over medium heat and add 2 teaspoons olive oil.

3. Sauté onions until soft, about 5 minutes, then add garlic and cook for 1 minute.

4. Transfer onion mixture into a large casserole dish.

5. Add potatoes, carrots, beans, zucchini, eggplant, tomatoes, oregano, salt, and pepper.

6. Sprinkle with remaining olive oil.

7. Cover with foil and bake until vegetables are tender, about 1 hour.

8. Garnish with fresh parsley and serve warm or room temperature.

This is the perfect comfort food for any family. Change up the vegetables seasonally, and add mashed potatoes to complete the meal. You can substitute a seven-bone roast for the meat. Just don't leave out the garlic cloves! They are the secret to making this such a heavenly roast.

Beef Stew with Root Vegetables

SERVES 6 to 8
PREP TIME: 20 MINUTES
COOK TIME: 3 HOURS

3-4 pound beef chuck roast
1 teaspoon salt
½ teaspoon freshly ground pepper
2 tablespoons extra virgin olive oil
2 sliced onions
2 bay leaves
6 whole cloves
¼ cup water
¼ cup red wine vinegar
3 carrots, peeled and cut into 1-inch
  pieces
3 parsnips, peeled and cut into 1-inch
  pieces
1 fennel bulb, chopped into 1-inch
  pieces
1 celery root, peeled and chopped into
  1-inch pieces
fresh parsley, chopped for garnish

1. Wash and trim fat off pot roast. Season all sides with salt and pepper.

2. Place 2 tablespoons of olive oil in a large Dutch oven or roasting pan and warm over medium heat.

3. Add pot roast and brown on all sides.

4. Add onions, bay leaves, cloves, water, and vinegar to roast.

5. Cover tightly and cook slowly for 2½ hours or until tender. Check often to add water to prevent from burning.

6. In the last 45 to 60 minutes add the remaining vegetables.

7. Continue cooking until vegetables are tender. Add parsley prior to serving.

Chapter 4
Marinating with Olive Oil

Marinating with Olive Oil

Marinades are usually acidic in nature. Originally made only with vinegar, marinades now include wine, fruit juices, buttermilk, olive oil and yogurt. The ingredients are immersed in the marinade for as little as a few hours or up to several days before cooking. Meats are marinated to improve their flavors and to make them moist and tender. Cutting the meat in smaller pieces reduces the marinating time. Marinades are not only for flavor but they also have health benefits. They reduce the carcinogenic substances formed on foods when you grill or fry at high temperatures.

Marinating Times:
Beef, Chicken, Game, Lamb, and Pork: 6 hours to overnight
Fish: 30 minutes for thin fillets, 1 hour for thicker cuts
Shellfish: 20 minutes

Tips on Marinating:

• Place the marinade in a plastic bag and add the meat. Refrigerate.
• Adding spices and herbs heightens the marinade flavor.
• Marinating times vary according to the food's texture. A tougher cut may require marinating up to 24 hours.
• Always cover and refrigerate marinated foods. Before cooking, remove as much of the marinade as possible and pat the meat dry, so it does not burn when cooked.

*C*hicken Kabobs with Cucumber-Mint Barley

*M*editerranean Vegetables in Olive Oil

*P*ork Tenderloin with Fresh Herbs and Bulgur

*S*ockeye Salmon with Spinach and Beet Greens

*N*ew York Strip Steak with Warm Cabbage Salad

These quick and easy lemon-marinated chicken kabobs can be made for any evening dinner. This satisfying and healthful combination will be a hit with your family and friends, especially for a summer meal on the patio.

Chicken Kabobs with Cucumber-Mint Barley

SERVES 6
PREP TIME: 15 MINUTES
MARINADE TIME: 3 HOURS
COOK TIME: 30 MINUTES

MARINADE

1 cup extra virgin olive oil
½ cup fresh lemon juice
1 teaspoon dried oregano
1 teaspoon salt
½ teaspoon freshly ground pepper

CHICKEN

6 chicken breasts, boneless and skinless
One 10-ounce box cherry tomatoes, washed
1-2 red onions, cut into 1-inch chunks
1 cup kalamata olives, pitted
2 lemons, cut into wedges

SALAD

1 pound barley
2½ cups water
2 cups tomatoes, peeled and chopped
2 cups cucumbers, peeled and chopped
2½ cups fresh parsley, chopped
½ cup mint, chopped
¼ cup green onions, thinly sliced
1 cup extra virgin olive oil
½ cup fresh lemon juice
½ teaspoon salt
¼ teaspoon freshly ground pepper

1. Combine all the marinade ingredients in a plastic bag.

2. Cut chicken into 1-inch cubes and place in the marinade. Seal and refrigerate for 3 hours or overnight.

3. Before grilling chicken, prepare barley. Place barley in a bowl and cover with cold water. Let stand for 30 minutes. Drain barley well.

4. Place barley and water in a medium saucepan and bring to a boil. Reduce heat to low and simmer for 40 to 50 minutes, until liquid has been absorbed.

5. Drain barley and rinse with cold water.

6. In a large bowl, toss barley with tomatoes, cucumbers, parsley, mint and green onions.

7. In a small bowl, whisk together oil and lemon juice.

8. Pour lemon dressing over barley, season with salt and pepper, and toss together. Refrigerate salad until ready to serve.

9. Soak bamboo skewers in water for 1 hour to prevent skewers from burning.

10. Skewer chicken pieces, alternating with tomatoes, onions, and olives.

11. Preheat the barbecue or oiled grill pan to medium-high heat. Cook until chicken juices are clear and chicken is browned, or until internal temperature is 165ºF.

12. Serve kabobs with barley and lemon wedges.

This brightly colored vegetable combo will dress up any cheese board for a dramatic presentation. Serve with cold cuts, breads, artisan cheeses, and pickles.

Mediterranean Vegetables in Olive Oil

YIELD: 5 TO 6 CUPS
PREP TIME: 15 MINUTES
MARINATE TIME: OVERNIGHT UP TO 3 WEEKS
COOK TIME: 30 MINUTES

VEGETABLES

3 red bell peppers
3 yellow bell peppers
½ cup fresh fava beans, or ½ cup canned small white beans
5 garlic cloves, sliced
1 cup mixed pitted olives, drained and halved
One 15-ounce can artichokes in water, drained and coarsely chopped
One 10-ounce box of white button mushrooms, cleaned and quartered

MARINADE

¾ cup extra virgin olive oil
⅓ cup sherry vinegar
½ teaspoon dried oregano
½ teaspoon dried basil
½ teaspoon salt
¼ teaspoon freshly ground pepper

1. Lightly rub bell peppers with olive oil. Place on a sheet pan and roast in a 400ºF oven until blistered. Place in a large bowl while hot and cover with plastic wrap for 15 minutes. Peel peppers and cut into strips. Return to bowl.

2. Place baby fava beans in a small pot of boiling water and cook until tender. Drain the water and cool. If using baby fava beans, you do not need to remove outer skin. If using larger fava beans, discard outer skin. If using canned white beans, rinse and drain.

3. Add beans, garlic, olives, artichokes, and mushrooms to the peppers.

4. To make marinade, whisk olive oil, vinegar, oregano, basil, salt, and pepper in a small bowl. Gently toss vegetables with marinade.

5. Place in a jar or deep bowl, cover, and refrigerate for up to 3 weeks. Turn often to allow marinade to coat the vegetables.

NOTE: Best when made the night before serving.

The savory combination of fresh parsley, thyme, and rosemary makes this pork tenderloin an exceptional dinner entrée, perfect for an evening of entertaining or a family-style dinner. Serve with the popular Mediterranean grain to introduce your dinner guests to this nutritious ingredient.

Pork Tenderloin with Fresh Herbs and Bulgur

SERVES 6
PREP TIME: 15 MINUTES
MARINATE TIME: 3 HOURS
COOK TIME: 30 MINUTES

MARINADE AND SAUCE

2 cups fresh parsley, chopped
½ cup fresh thyme, chopped
¼ cup fresh rosemary, finely chopped
zest from 1 lemon
¼ cup fresh lemon juice
3 garlic cloves, chopped
1 tablespoon salt
½ cup extra virgin olive oil

PORK

Two 1-pound boneless pork tenderloin
2 teaspoons extra virgin olive oil

BULGUR

1 tablespoon extra virgin olive oil
2 cups cherry tomatoes, halved
½ cup dry sun-dried tomatoes, minced
2 teaspoons salt, divided
2 garlic cloves, minced
1½ cups bulgur
2 cups water
¼ cup fresh lemon juice
½ cup toasted pine nuts
½ teaspoon freshly ground pepper

1. Place marinade ingredients, except olive oil, in a food processor.

2. Process for 10 seconds then slowly add olive oil. Divide marinade in half.

3. Reserve half the marinade to serve with pork tenderloin. Place other half of marinade in a bag and add pork to marinate. Seal the bag and refrigerate for 3 hours or up to overnight.

4. Preheat oven to 400ºF.

5. Add 2 teaspoons of olive oil in a large oven-safe sauté pan and bring to medium-high heat.

6. Remove both pork tenderloins from bag and place in the pan. Brown evenly on all sides.

7. Place hot pan in oven and roast for 30 minutes or until internal temperature of roast reaches 160ºF.

8. While the pork cooks, make the bulgur. Add olive oil in a sauté pan and heat to medium.

9. Add cherry tomatoes and cook for 5 minutes.

10. Add sun-dried tomatoes, and season with 1 teaspoon salt.

11. Reduce heat to medium-low, add garlic and bulgur, and sauté for 2 minutes.

12. Add 2 cups of water and bring to a boil. Reduce heat and simmer for 20 to 25 minutes.

13 Fluff with a fork and stir in lemon juice and pine nuts. Season with last teaspoon of salt and pepper.

14. Transfer pork to a serving platter and slice. Drizzle reserved herb sauce over the pork and serve.

For an elegant yet simple dinner, marinate salmon in wine and lemon and serve with a healthful serving of greens. Do not marinate the salmon for more than 60 minutes or the marinade will begin to "cook" the fish.

Sockeye Salmon with Spinach and Beet Greens

SERVES 4
PREP TIME: 15 MINUTES
MARINATE TIME: 30 MINUTES
COOK TIME: 30 MINUTES

SALMON

One 3-pound sockeye salmon fillet
3 thin lemon slices

MARINADE

¼ cup extra virgin olive oil
¼ cup white wine
1 teaspoon lemon juice
½ tablespoon Dijon mustard
2 garlic cloves, chopped
¼ cup fresh basil, chopped
½ teaspoon fresh parsley, chopped
¼ teaspoon salt
¼ teaspoon freshly ground pepper

GREENS

1 teaspoon extra virgin olive oil
2 garlic cloves, chopped
1 bunch beet greens, washed and
  coarsely chopped
1 bunch spinach, washed and coarsely
  chopped

DRESSING

2 teaspoons extra virgin olive oil
juice from 2 lemons
1 teaspoon salt
½ teaspoon freshly ground pepper

1. Place salmon in an oiled baking dish.

2. Mix marinade ingredients together and pour marinade on the fish. Let fish marinate for 30 minutes.

3. Preheat oven to 400ºF.

4. Place lemon slices on top of salmon.

5. Bake in oven for 15 to 20 minutes until fish flakes easily with a fork or has an internal temperature of 140ºF.

6. To prepare greens, add 1 teaspoon of olive oil to a large sauté pan and heat to medium. Add garlic and stir.

7. Add greens and sauté until wilted, about 5 minutes.

8. To make dressing place lemon juice, salt, and pepper in a small bowl. Whisk together. Slowly whisk in 2 teaspoons olive oil until emulsified.

9. Mix dressing with greens.

10. Place greens and salmon on a large platter and serve.

This marinade has bold flavors often needed to enhance the steak. Feel free to substitute a T-bone or Porterhouse steak for this recipe. You may need to double the marinade if using several larger steaks.

New York Strip Steak with Warm Cabbage Salad

SERVES 4
PREP TIME: 15 MINUTES
MARINATE TIME: 3 TO 12 HOURS
COOK TIME: 25 MINUTES

STEAK AND MARINADE

2 New York steaks, fat trimmed
½ cup extra virgin olive oil
¼ cup red wine vinegar
2 garlic cloves, chopped
1 teaspoon dried oregano
½ teaspoon salt
¼ teaspoon freshly ground pepper

SALAD

2 slices bacon, finely chopped
⅓ cup diced leeks
2 garlic cloves, minced
⅓ cup vegetable stock
3 tablespoons white wine vinegar
2 pounds savoy cabbage, sliced
2 bok choy, chopped
12 cherry tomatoes
1 tablespoon fresh parsley, chopped

1. Place all marinade ingredients in a large plastic bag or bowl and whisk until blended.

2. Pour marinade into a plastic bag, add steaks, seal the bag, and marinate for 3 hours or up to overnight.

3. Place steaks on a barbecue or inside grill and cook to desired doneness. Test with instant thermometer: for rare 120-130ºF, for medium 135-145ºF, for well done 170ºF.

4. Remove steaks and cover with foil. While steak is resting, prepare warm cabbage salad.

5. Cook bacon in a large skillet until crisp. Drain and place on paper towel.

6. In the same pan sauté leeks and garlic until leeks soften, about 3 minutes.

7. Add stock, vinegar, cabbage, and bok choy to the pan and cook until cabbage is limp and tender, about 3 minutes.

8. Remove from heat and place salad on a serving platter.

9. Cut steak into slices and place over the cabbage salad.

10. Garnish with tomatoes, parsley, bacon, and serve.

Chapter 5
Healthy Steamed Recipes Enhanced with Olive Oil

Healthy Steamed Recipes Enhanced with Olive Oil

Steaming is a common cooking method in which water is brought to a rolling boil, creating steam. Food is placed in a basket or tray above the boiling water so it is not in direct contact with it. Instead, the steam passes through the steam basket and surrounds the food, cooking it. A lid is placed over the food and pot, keeping the steam trapped inside and continuously cooking the food.

There are multiple ways to cook with steam. A metal basket can be inserted into the bottom of a pot that rests inches above the boiling water. Stackable Chinese bamboo baskets can also be used. Small metal stands that raise the food above the water are another option. All of these methods steam food over the stove with a pot of boiling water. You can also steam in the oven by wrapping your meat and vegetables in parchment paper. The moisture from the food becomes trapped in the sealed parchment container, thus providing steam that cooks the food while it bakes.

Steamed food is typically healthier, requires less fat, and results in a moist meal that retains more of its nutrients compared to other cooking methods. So, if foods prepared by steaming are healthier and have less fat, why add fat by using olive oil? Although olive oil does contain healthy fats that our bodies need, the main reason to add olive oil to your steamed food is to enhance flavor.

In this chapter, the foods are steamed using multiple methods. Sometimes water is added, other times the liquid released by the food item being steamed aids in the steaming process. The meat or vegetable being steamed is typically coated with olive oil to provide more flavor to an otherwise bland-tasting dish.

Tips on Steaming:

- Wrap meats in an edible lettuce or cabbage leaf, or set into either a parchment or foil envelope.
- The meat should be placed in a single layer to insure even cooking.
- The pot should contain enough water so it does not dry out as steam escapes.
- Keep lids tight on the pot, and heat over high heat so the pot's inside atmosphere is saturated with vapor.
- Herbs and spices can be used to infuse the item.

Basmati Rice with Potatoes, Dill, and Saffron

Stuffed Grape Leaves with Brown Rice, Kale, and Fresh Herbs

Mussels with Lemon Saffron Broth

Baby Beets and Brussels Sprouts Salad

Salmon with Olive Oil in Parchment (Saumon en Papillote)

Basmati rice is a staple food for most Middle Eastern countries. This recipe is Persian, uses dill, and is dairy-free. And don't forget the irresistible potato crust!

Basmati Rice with Potatoes, Dill, and Saffron

SERVES 4 TO 6
PREP TIME: 10 MINUTES
COOK TIME: 1 HOUR

8 cups water
1¼ teaspoons salt, divided
2 cups white basmati rice
6-7 saffron threads
3 tablespoons extra virgin olive oil, divided
8 ounces russet potatoes, peeled and sliced into ¼-inch rounds
½ cup (4 ounces) dried dill

1. Pour water in a large nonstick pot, stir in 1 teaspoon of salt, cover, and bring to a boil over high heat.

2. While waiting for water to boil, place rice in a bowl and cover with cold water.

3. Stir rice with your hands to remove dirt and extra starch. Pour water out. Rinse and drain two more times. Set aside.

4. Using a mortar and pestle, grind the saffron. Add 1 tablespoon hot water from the boiling water and pour it into saffron. Set aside and reserve.

5. When the water comes to a boil, add drained rice. Cook until the rice is half done and still crunchy in the center, about 6 minutes. Pour rice through a fine mesh colander to drain.

6. Return pot to the stove and place over medium heat. Add 2 tablespoons of olive oil to coat the bottom. Place potato slices in one layer lining the bottom of the pot. Season potatoes with ¼ teaspoon of salt.

7. Using a spatula, gently scatter scoopfuls of drained rice over the potatoes, just covering the potatoes. Do not press down on rice or tap the spatula against the pot. You want to insure space and gaps within the rice for steam to pass. This will also keep rice from turning to mush.

8. Generously scatter dried dill over the first layer of rice, until mostly covered. Continue adding layers of rice and dill until everything is back in the pot.

9. Using the handle of your spatula, gently press a hole through the center of the rice to the bottom of the pot for steam to pass through. Pour last tablespoon of olive oil evenly over rice. Pour reserved saffron water over the top as well.

10. Cover the pot with a clean kitchen towel (or two sheets of paper towels) and then cover with the lid. Wrap the rest of the towel over the lid. The towel will catch the extra steam and prevent condensation from dripping down back into the rice. This will keep rice from getting sticky.

11. Reduce heat to simmer and steam rice until done, about 45 to 60 minutes.

12. To serve rice, place an inverted plate over your pot and carefully flip the pot and the plate together. Gently remove the pot so potato crust is on top of rice. Alternatively, reserve the top scoop of rice, then scatter remaining rice in your serving platter, adding reserved rice for the top. Remove potato crust and place along the side of your serving platter. If your crust is not golden brown, continue cooking potato slices over medium-high heat for several more minutes, checking often to prevent them from burning.

Persians call them "dolmeh" while Greeks call them "dolmata." Whatever you call them, you will declare them delicious! Traditionally made with white rice, these grape leaves are stuffed with nutty brown basmati rice.

Stuffed Grape Leaves with Brown Rice, Kale, and Fresh Herbs

YIELD: 36 DOLMEH
PREP TIME: 45 MINUTES
COOK TIME: 1 HOUR

- 36-40 large grape leaves
- 1 cup uncooked brown basmati rice (or 4 cups of cooked)
- 2¼ cups water (divided)
- ¾ teaspoon salt (divided)
- 1½ ounces kale, finely chopped
- ¼ cup fresh dill, loosely packed
- ½ cup fresh parsley, loosely packed
- ½ cup fresh mint, loosely packed
- 3 ounces dried cranberries
- 2 tablespoons extra virgin olive oil
- ¼ cup pomegranate concentrate
- ¼ teaspoon freshly ground pepper
- ½ cup lemon juice

1. For fresh grape leaves, choose tender ones, blanch in boiling water for 2 to 3 minutes, drain in a colander, and rinse with cold water. For brined grape leaves, carefully unfold, rinse with cold water, and drain in a colander.

2. If using cooked rice, skip this step. In a small pot add 2 cups of water, uncooked brown rice, and ¼ teaspoon of salt. Cover and bring to boil. Reduce heat to low and cook until water is gone and rice is cooked, about 45 minutes.

3. Finely chop herbs and combine with warm rice in a bowl. Mix in kale, 1 tablespoon of olive oil, pomegranate concentrate, and dried cranberries.

4. Coat the bottom of a 4-quart non-stick pot with 1 tablespoon of olive oil.

5. Working with one grape leaf at a time, spread grape leaf flat on your work surface, with the vein side up. Pinch off any stems.

6. Drop into the center of your grape leaf 1 to 2 tablespoons of rice filling. Depending on the size of your grape leaves, the amount of filling can vary. Grape leaves the size of an adult hand should hold up to 2 tablespoons of filling.

7. Starting at the bottom of the leaf, pull up the lower part of the grape leaf to cover the filling, tucking the tip under the filling.

8. Keeping the dolmeh tight, but not pulling so hard that you tear the grape leaf, fold the left flap of the leaf over the center, followed by folding over the right flap.

9. Tightly roll the dolmeh towards the top of the grape leaf. See pictures to the left for more guidance.

10. Once completely rolled, place dolmeh, seam side down, into the oiled pot.

11. Continue rolling the rest of the grape leaves until all of the filling is finished. Layer dolmeh snugly together into the pot, making a second and third layer as needed.

12. Combine ¼ cup water and lemon juice, and pour over dolmeh.

13. Place a plate on top of the dolmeh. This keeps the dolmeh from expanding and opening up while cooking. Cover pot and cook over low heat for 1 hour.

14. Dolmeh can be served immediately warm or at room temperature. Or refrigerate dolmeh in an airtight container for up to 3 days. Serve with a side of plain yogurt (optional).

Next time you are watching the big game, flex your muscles with steamed mussels. This is an easy appetizer or a wonderful meal for two. The mussels are steamed in a combination of wine, lemon juice and olive oil. Make sure you have plenty of bread to soak up the delectable broth.

Mussels with Lemon Saffron Broth

SERVES 2
PREP TIME: 10 MINUTES
COOK TIME: 15 MINUTES

1 pound mussels
½ cup extra virgin olive oil
½ cup white wine
¼ cup lemon juice
2 garlic cloves, crushed
⅛ teaspoon ground saffron
zest from 1 lemon, grated
½ teaspoon salt
¼ teaspoon freshly ground pepper
1 tablespoon fresh thyme leaves

1. Rinse mussels well under cold water, scrubbing off any beards (the fibers attached to the shell). Discard any that have broken shells or are open wide. Set mussels aside.

2. In a large skillet whisk together the remaining ingredients, except for thyme, over medium heat until steamy, about 10 minutes.

3. Add mussels and cover. Cook until all of the mussels open, about 5 minutes. Discard any unopened mussels. Season sauce with salt and pepper.

4. Top with fresh thyme and serve with bread or pasta.

NOTE: This recipe can easily be doubled for larger crowds.

Baby beets are the perfect size for steaming, and perfectly sweet too! And by placing the olive oil-coated beets in a shallow bowl over a bamboo steamer, you can collect their juices to make into a vinaigrette. Save the beet greens, as they are delicious when eaten raw or steamed.

Baby Beets and Brussels Sprouts Salad

SERVES 2
PREP TIME: 15 MINUTES
COOK TIME: 30 MINUTES

SALAD

3 baby beets, washed, trimmed, and peeled
1 tablespoon extra virgin olive oil
8 large Brussels sprouts, thinly sliced or shredded
2 tablespoons feta cheese, crumbled
½ teaspoon fresh dill

VINAIGRETTE

¼ cup extra virgin olive oil
¼ cup red wine vinegar
1 garlic clove, minced
½ teaspoon salt
¼ teaspoon freshly ground pepper
reserved beet juice from steaming

1. Place beets in a small, heatproof shallow bowl.

2. Fill a wok or a pot large enough to hold a bamboo steamer with 2-inches of water. Place the bamboo steamer into the wok. Place the shallow bowl holding beets into the steamer and cover. See picture on page 79. The shallow bowl will collect the juice "sweating" from beets. You will use this juice in the vinaigrette.

3. Bring water to a boil and steam until beets are fork tender, 35 to 45 minutes.

4. Carefully remove the basket from the steam and allow beets to cool to room temperature, about 1 hour. Chill until ready to serve.

5. Strain beet juice and blend with other vinaigrette ingredients.

6. Divide sliced Brussels sprouts on two serving plates.

7. Slice beets in half and divide among the two plates. Top with feta and fresh dill, and serve with vinaigrette.

You can also steam your food in the oven using parchment paper. This technique works well for fish and chicken. Use any of your favorite vegetables, such as broccoli, mushrooms, or asparagus. Double the recipe, make an assembly line for your next party, and your guests will customize their own entrée.

Salmon with Olive Oil in Parchment (Saumon en Papillote)

SERVES 2-4
PREP TIME: 15 MINUTES
COOK TIME: 20 MINUTES

2 salmon fillets, 5 ounces each
  or 1 large fillet
1 tablespoon extra virgin olive oil
⅛ teaspoon salt
⅛ teaspoon lemon pepper
4 lemon slices
8 asparagus stalks
1 small shallot, sliced
1 tablespoon capers
½ teaspoon fresh chives, finely chopped

1. Preheat oven to 450ºF.

2. Place each salmon fillet in the center of a 16-inch x 12-inch piece of parchment paper.

3. Brush salmon with olive oil and season with salt and pepper. Divide slices of lemon and place on top of each fillet.

4. Add asparagus, shallot, capers, and chives to top of each fillet.

5. Pull the two long ends of parchment paper straight up, fold ends together, and continue to roll and crimp until tightly sealed. Roll and crimp the smaller ends of the parchment paper until your package is wrapped.

6. Place fish packets onto a baking sheet and bake for 15 minutes.

7. Remove from oven and allow packets to rest for 5 minutes before opening.

8. Place packet on your plate and open slowly and carefully to avoid burning your hands from the hot steam.

Chapter 6
Baking with Olive Oil

Baking with Olive Oil

live oil is a terrific choice for lowering saturated fats in your baked goods. Because of the multiple choices of flavors and intensities of olive oil, you must find one that will match well with whatever you are baking. This is best done by tasting the olive oil on its own. This choice is typically a personal preference.

Olive oil is not just for baking muffins. You can also make breads, cakes, scones, and cookies. For recipes that include a vegetable oil, replace it with the same amount of olive oil. The ratio here is 1:1. When substituting butter in baked recipes, however, a better ratio is 4:3. So, for every cup of butter used, replace it with ¾ cup of olive oil. A full chart with conversions can be found on page 128.

Not all baking recipes will result in success when you substitute olive oil for butter. For example, any recipes that must stay solid at room temperature, such as cake frosting, will not work with olive oil.

Remember, when baking with olive oil, you want the oil you choose to enhance the flavor of your creation. A low-quality oil can leave an unpleasant aftertaste, so choose an oil that you would enjoy drizzled on your salad or your bread. If you do not like the taste of the oil in its raw form, do not add it to your recipe.

Flavored olive oils can enhance your baked goods, too. Fruity flavors are wonderful in sweet treats like cakes, cookies, and pies. Choose an herb or garlic flavored olive oil for your breads and other savory baked recipes.

Whole Wheat Scones with Blueberries and Lavender

Kalamata Olive Bread with Rosemary

Olive Oil Sugar Cookies

Dark Chocolate Olive Oil Cake with Strawberries

Apple Lattice Pie with Olive Oil Crust

Olive Oil Almond Cookies with Rosewater and Cardamom

Typically, scones are made with cold butter and white flour. These whole wheat scones are not only moist and crumbly, but also bursting with flavor from fresh blueberries and lavender. They are perfect to enjoy with your morning tea or for an afternoon snack.

Whole Wheat Scones with Blueberries and Lavender

SERVES 6
PREP TIME: 15 MINUTES
COOK TIME: 30 MINUTES

2 cups whole wheat flour
⅓ cup fresh lavender, loosely packed
1 tablespoon baking powder
⅛ teaspoon salt
¼ cup raw sugar plus ½ teaspoon
   to top scones
⅓ cup extra virgin olive oil
¼ cup nonfat Greek yogurt, plain
¼ cup low-fat milk
1 large egg
1 tablespoon wheat bran
4 ounces fresh blueberries

1. Preheat oven to 400ºF. Line a baking sheet with parchment paper or use a silicone baking mat.

2. In a food processor, pulse to combine flour, lavender, baking powder, and salt. Pulse ¼ cup raw sugar with the flour mixture.

3. Pulse and pour olive oil into the mixture until crumbly.

4. In a small bowl, whisk together yogurt, milk, and egg. Pulse and combine egg mixture with the rest of the ingredients.

5. Turn crumbly dough onto a lightly floured surface or silicone baking mat and press dough together to form a circle or rectangle ½-inch thick. Press wheat bran onto all sides of the dough.

6. Spread most of the blueberries onto half of the dough and fold the empty half over it.

7. Press any runaway and remaining blueberries onto the top of the dough.

8. Cut into 6 equal pieces, garnish tops with ½ teaspoon raw sugar, and transfer scones onto prepared baking sheet.

9. Bake for 12 to 15 minutes, until golden. Allow scones to cool on the baking sheet for 5 minutes. Serve warm or place on a cooling rack to cool completely.

NOTE: If you do not have fresh lavender, substitute with dried culinary lavender, available in specialty food stores.

The smell of freshly baked bread will call everyone to the table. This olive bread will be quickly devoured, whether you are eating it plain or decide to dip it in your favorite olive oil and balsamic vinegar.

Kalamata Olive Bread with Rosemary

YIELD: 10-INCH ROUND LOAF
PREP TIME: 3 HOURS, 30 MINUTES
COOK TIME: 20 MINUTES

¾ cup warm water (100ºF)
½ teaspoon quick active dry yeast
2 cups unbleached all-purpose flour, plus approximately ¼ cup more for kneading
1 tablespoon sugar
1 tablespoon fresh rosemary, coarsely chopped
½ teaspoon salt
2 tablespoons extra virgin olive oil, plus 1 teaspoon to brush on the top
⅔ cup coarsely chopped kalamata olives, pitted

1. In a small bowl or measuring cup mix together the yeast and warm water. Let it rest for 5 to 7 minutes until yeast is foamy.

2. In a larger bowl whisk together flour, sugar, rosemary, and salt. Create a well in the center of the bowl and pour in 2 tablespoons olive oil and foamy yeast mixture.

3. Using a fork at first, start mixing dry ingredients into wet ingredients until a coarse dough is formed. Using well-floured hands, continue to mix dough until a rough ball is formed.

4. Turn dough onto a lightly floured work surface, and knead adding in the chopped olives as you work. Continue to sprinkle in more flour (up to ¼ cup) while you knead until dough is smooth and not sticky, about 10 minutes.

5. Place dough ball onto a baking sheet with a silicone baking mat, cover with a clean kitchen towel, and place in a warm area to rise until it doubles in size, about 2 to 3 hours.

6. Preheat oven to 400ºF.

7. Remove the towel and cut two lines into dough. Brush with 1 teaspoon of olive oil and bake until bread is golden, about 15 to 20 minutes.

You won't miss the butter in these delicate cookies. Perfect for any holiday, and they can be cut into any shape. Use a fruit flavored olive oil and you won't need any icing. Or, try an herb flavored olive oil for a touch of savory.

Olive Oil Sugar Cookies

YIELD 36 COOKIES
PREP TIME: 30 MINUTES
COOK TIME: 7 MINUTES PER BATCH

2½ cups all-purpose flour
½ teaspoon baking powder
¼ teaspoon salt
¾ cup extra virgin olive oil
1 cup sugar
1 egg
1 tablespoon milk

1. Preheat oven to 350°F. Line a baking sheet with parchment paper or use a silicone baking mat.

2. In a small bowl whisk together flour, baking powder, and salt.

3. In a larger bowl whisk together olive oil, sugar, egg, and milk until combined.

4. In batches, whisk dry ingredients into wet ingredients.

5. Knead dough by hand for 5 minutes until smooth, and form a ball.

6. Divide dough in half, set aside, and cover one half with a clean towel. Flatten other half of the dough to a disk, and roll out between two sheets of parchment paper until ¼-inch thick.

7. Cut cookies with a 2-inch circle cookie cutter or other shape.

8. Using a thin off-set spatula, transfer cookie shapes onto prepared baking sheet. If dough is too sticky, dip spatula into flour first.

9. Bake for 7 minutes until lightly golden. Do not brown or cookies will be too hard.

10. Allow cookies to rest on the baking sheet for 2 minutes. Then, using a spatula, transfer to a cooling rack to cool thoroughly.

11. Repeat with the remaining half of dough.

NOTE: For drier climates, you may find that dough will not stick together. If this is the case, add an extra 1 to 2 tablespoons of milk.

Moist and filled with extra chocolaty goodness, this cake is sure to please kids of all ages. Choose either a fruity or neutral olive oil, depending on your personal palate.

Dark Chocolate Olive Oil Cake with Strawberries

YIELD: 1 9-INCH ROUND CAKE
PREP TIME: 20 MINUTES
COOK TIME: 45 MINUTES

1 cup unbleached all-purpose flour
½ cup unsweetened dark cocoa powder
2 teaspoons baking powder
⅛ teaspoon salt
¾ cup granulated sugar
¾ cup nonfat Greek yogurt, plain
3 large eggs
1 teaspoon vanilla extract
½ cup extra virgin olive oil
¾ cup dark chocolate chips
8 large strawberries, halved with the tops removed

1. Preheat oven to 350ºF. Apply nonstick spray to a 9-inch round baking pan, and line bottom with parchment paper.

2. In a medium-sized bowl whisk together flour, cocoa powder, baking powder, and salt.

3. In a large bowl, mix sugar, yogurt, eggs, vanilla, and olive oil together until combined.

4. In batches, mix flour mixture into yogurt and stir until combined. Stir in chocolate chips, then pour cake batter into the prepared pan.

5. Arrange strawberry halves over the top of the cake.

6. Bake for 40 to 45 minutes or until a toothpick inserted into the center comes out clean.

7. Allow cake to cool on the pan for 15 minutes; then gently run a knife along the side of cake. Carefully remove cake from the pan and transfer to a cooling rack to cool completely.

8. Serve alone, dusted with powdered sugar, or add a scoop of vanilla ice cream.

*T*op your cake with other fruits like raspberries, peaches, oranges and pears.

Olive oil pie crust? Tender, moist, and flakey, you may never go back to a butter crust again!

Apple Lattice Pie with Olive Oil Crust

SERVES 8 TO 12
PREP TIME: 35 MINUTES
COOK TIME: 25 MINUTES

CRUST

4 cups all-purpose flour, plus up to ¼ cup extra for rolling out the dough
10 teaspoons granulated sugar
1 teaspoon salt
1 cup plus 2 tablespoons extra virgin olive oil
½ cup water

FILLING

3 pounds baking apples, peeled and cored
¼ cup light brown sugar, packed
1 tablespoon lemon juice
1 tablespoon all-purpose flour
¼ teaspoon ground cinnamon
⅛ teaspoon ground cloves

EGG WASH

1 large egg
1 teaspoon water

1. Preheat oven to 400°F.

2. Cut apples in half. Cut halved apples into thin slices. Add apples into a mixing bowl, and gently mix with the rest of the filling ingredients until all apple slices are coated. Reserve apples.

3. In a large mixing bowl add dry crust ingredients, and stir with a fork to combine.

4. Stir in olive oil, and mix with a fork until dough resembles small pebbles. Stir in water, 1 tablespoon at a time, until dough starts to stick together.

5. Turn dough onto a lightly floured large silicone mat or parchment paper and form into a flattened disk. Remove and reserve ⅓ of the dough for lattice top.

6. Place another sheet of parchment paper over the remaining ⅔ of the dough, and slowly roll dough out until an 11-inch circle is formed, approximately ¼-inch thick.

7. Dip a thin off-set spatula into flour, and slide it under the bottom of dough. Continue this process of dipping the spatula into flour and sliding it under dough until all of the bottom of the pie dough has been covered with flour.

8. Slowly peel back the top sheet of parchment paper.

9. Carefully invert dough and gently place over a 9-inch pie dish that is 1-inch deep. You do not need to grease the pie dish. The exposed dough will be facing

down into the pie dish, while the top of the dough will still have the top parchment sheet over it.

10. Gently press dough into the bottom and sides of the pie pan.

11. Slowly peel off the top parchment paper when done. Press and fold the excess dough under itself to form a thick trim. Pinch trim or press with a fork, as desired, for decorative touch.

12. Roll out reserved dough as you did the first. Gently peel off the top parchment paper.

13. Using a butter knife dipped in flour and a ruler, slice long strips, approximately ½-inch wide.

14. Fill pie shell with reserved apple filling. Using an off-set spatula, gently peel, one at a time, the rectangle strips off the parchment paper.

15. For the lattice top, place every other strip over the filling, and weave the lattice by folding every other strip back and laying down another strip in the perpendicular direction. Fold the strips back across and repeat until finished.

16. Whisk together egg wash ingredients in a small bowl. Using a pastry brush, brush egg wash over lattice top crust and crust edges.

17. Bake until crust is golden, approximately 25 minutes. Allow to cool at least 1 hour before serving.

This little cookie packs a big crunch. Use a nutty flavored olive oil to bring out the almond goodness and highlight the hints of rosewater and cardamom.

Olive Oil Almond Cookies with Rosewater and Cardamom

YIELD: 40 COOKIES
PREP TIME: 15 MINUTES
COOK TIME: 12 MINUTES PER BATCH

1 cup almond meal
¾ cup unbleached all-purpose flour
½ cup light brown sugar, packed
½ teaspoon salt
½ teaspoon ground cardamom
½ cup extra virgin olive oil
1 tablespoon rosewater
1 teaspoon vanilla extract

1. Preheat oven to 375ºF. Line a baking sheet with parchment paper or use a silicone baking mat.

2. In a medium size bowl, whisk together dry ingredients.

3. In a small bowl, whisk together wet ingredients.

4. Pour wet ingredients into dry and mix until incorporated.

5. Scoop out 1 tablespoon of dough, flatten it into a circle about ¼-inch thick, and place onto the prepared baking sheet. Continue doing this with the rest of the dough until baking sheet is full, spacing the cookies about 1-inch apart.

6. Bake for 12 minutes or until the edges are golden. Allow cookies to cool on the baking sheet for 5 minutes, then transfer to a cooling rack to cool completely.

NOTE: Rosewater can be found in Middle Eastern markets. If you cannot find it, substitute with 2 teaspoons of almond extract.

Chapter 7
Other Cooking Techniques Using Olive Oil

Infusing with Olive Oil

$\mathcal{O}$ils infused with garlic, fresh herbs, dried herbs, or hot peppers are called flavored or infused oils. Adding spices and herbs to extra virgin olive oil adds interesting flavors and enhances the oils. Usually the herb is bruised before being added to the oil. To bruise, gently rub a few sprigs of the herb in your hands. This step will make it easier for the oil to penetrate and for the aromas to escape.

Important: Commercially prepared flavored olive oils are usually safe to keep and use for a long time. Homemade oils are not. If you make your own infused oils, make up a small batch, keep it refrigerated, and use it up within 2 to 3 days.

$\mathcal{T}$ips on Infusing:

• Always start with clean sterilized bottles and lids.
• Infused oils can replace butters on bread and pastas and have a multitude of uses in the kitchen.
• Oil is heated before the herb or spice is added to remove any bacteria present.
• Toast whole spices, nuts, and seeds before grinding and adding to the oil for a more complex flavor.
• Flavored oils can be used to finish a dish, or to make into sauces, dressings, or marinades.
• If the oil becomes cloudy, discard the entire product.

Triple-Herb Infused Olive Oil

In a sterilized bottle, add one rosemary sprig, two oregano sprigs, and two thyme sprigs. Heat approximately 2 cups of olive oil to a simmer for 10 minutes. Bring the oil back to room temperature and pour into your bottle. Refrigerate immediately and use up within 2 to 3 days.

Vanilla and Cinnamon Infused Olive Oil

In a sterilized bottle, add two vanilla beans and a cinnamon stick. Heat approximately 2 cups of olive oil to a simmer for 10 minutes. Bring the oil back to room temperature and pour into your bottle. Refrigerate immediately and use up within 2 to 3 days.

Garlic and Peppercorn Infused Olive Oil

In a small sterilized jar, add 6 to 8 garlic cloves and 10 peppercorns. Heat approximately 2 cups of olive oil to a simmer for 10 minutes. Bring the oil back to room temperature and pour into your bottle. Refrigerate immediately and use up within 2 to 3 days.

Baby Rose Bud and Clove Infused Olive Oil

In a sterilized bottle, add clean, dried rose buds and whole cloves. Heat approximately 2 cups of the olive oil to a simmer for 10 minutes. Bring the oil back to room temperature and pour into your bottle. Refrigerate immediately and use up within 2 to 3 days.

Preserving with Olive Oil

*M*aking confit is the simplest technique you will find in this book. The term confit is derived from an old French phrase meaning "preserving food." In the past, this was the most commonly used method for preserving food. Today, the two terms "confit" and "preserving" are used interchangeably. Confit refers to a cooking method of immersing a vegetable or fruit in liquid over a low simmer temperature, cooking it slowly until it reaches a rich and silky texture. The word "preserve" today means for food to last one week or less. For a longer shelf life, you must go through the canning process to prevent any bad bacteria from entering your preserved food.

Most modern versions of confit are refrigerated for safety reasons and eaten within the week. Getting started is very easy when it comes to confit. Always begin with clean, sanitized glass jars and lids. Use clean utensils when removing the vegetables. Refrigerate the jar immediately after use.

Oven-Dried Tomatoes with Olive Oil

YIELD: 16-OUNCE JAR
PREP TIME: 10 MINUTES
COOK TIME: 30 MINUTES

8 plum tomatoes, halved lengthwise
3 tablespoons extra virgin olive oil,
   plus up to 1 cup more for jars
1½ teaspoons dried oregano
½ teaspoon salt
⅛ teaspoon freshly ground pepper
2 sprigs fresh oregano or basil
3 fresh rosemary sprigs
2 garlic cloves, peeled

1. Preheat oven to 300ºF. Line a baking sheet with parchment paper or silicone baking mat.

2. In a large bowl, add olive oil and tomatoes and gently mix to coat tomatoes.

3. Season tomatoes with dried oregano, salt, and pepper.

4. Place tomatoes cut side up on the baking sheet. Bake in oven for 3 to 4 hours, turning tomatoes over after 2 hours.

5. Remove from oven when tomatoes have lost most of their moisture. Larger tomatoes will take more time to cook. Set aside to cool to room temperature.

6. Add oregano, fresh rosemary, and garlic into 1 or 2 mason jars. Place tomatoes snugly into the jars.

7. Cover with olive oil, seal the jar tightly and refrigerate.

8. Tomatoes will keep in the refrigerator for up to one week.

Use the preserved
vegetables in salads, pastas,
sauces, and vinaigrettes.
Serve as an appetizer with
fresh bread.

The sweet garlic cloves are preserved in olive oil and would pair beautifully with roasted eggplant or bell peppers. Add them to your favorite pasta sauce, and save the oil to drizzle over bread or roasted vegetables.

Garlic Confit in Olive Oil

YIELD: 1 8-OUNCE JAR
PREP TIME: 15 MINUTES
COOK TIME: 45 MINUTES

1 cup garlic cloves, peeled
1 dried bay leaf
2 sprigs fresh mint
⅛ teaspoon kosher salt
3 peppercorns
1 cup extra virgin olive oil

1. Place a small saucepan on low heat and add peeled garlic, bay leaf, mint, salt, and peppercorns.

2. Cover garlic with olive oil and simmer.

3. Cook on low until garlic is soft and golden, but not browned, approximately 30 to 45 minutes. If garlic burns, you must discard entire batch of garlic and oil and start again.

4. Once golden, remove from heat and cool to room temperature.

5. Transfer garlic and olive oil into a sterilized jar, and seal tightly with the lid. Refrigerate up to one week.

Experiment with different combinations of herbs and spices.

• oregano and basil
• parsley and rosemary
• dried chiles with cilantro
• cloves, cinnamon stick, and nutmeg
• mustard, fennel seeds, and peppercorns

Whipping with Olive Oil

Whipping olive oil by hand guarantees a thick and creamy dressing for your sandwiches. The key to successfully whipping the olive oil is to start slowly, adding the oil drop by drop. Make sure all of the ingredients are at room temperature. Use an olive oil that is mild in flavor. By adding fresh herbs and garlic, you can customize the mayonnaise to your taste.

Homemade Olive Oil Mayonnaise

YIELD: 1¼ CUPS
PREP TIME: 30 MINUTES

1 large egg yolk, at room temperature
1 teaspoon Dijon mustard
1 teaspoon fresh lemon juice
1 cup extra virgin olive oil, divided
¼ teaspoon salt
⅛ teaspoon freshly ground pepper

1. Place egg yolk in a medium bowl. Using a whisk, beat until light and fluffy.

2. Whisk in mustard and lemon juice.

3. Slowly whisk in ¼ cup olive oil until thickened. Do not rush as you continue adding the remaining olive oil, drop by drop, until mayonnaise completely thickens.

4. Season with salt and pepper.

5. Cover and chill. Refrigerate for up to 5 days.

VARIATIONS:

Herbal: add 2 tablespoons of freshly chopped chives, parsley, tarragon, or oregano.

Horseradish: add 2 tablespoons of spicy horseradish just before serving.

Garlic: add 1 crushed garlic clove with the egg yolks.

NOTE: Because of a slight risk of bacterial poisoning, the USDA advises against the consumption of raw eggs by pregnant women, young children, and anyone having a weakened immune system or other compromised health issues. Pasteurized fresh eggs are commercially available and safe to use.

Blending with Olive Oil

*M*ost often when blending with olive oil, the end product is an emulsified sauce called a "vinaigrette." The word "vinaigrette" comes from the French word for vinegar. Vinaigrettes are generally used for salad dressings, toppings for vegetables, or dressings for rice and grain salads.

*T*ips on Blending:

• The proportions for these vinaigrettes are 2 parts olive oil to 1 part vinegar.
• The vinegar and salt are combined first to dissolve the salt.
• Herbs, mustards, and other flavorings are added before dressing the salad.
• The salad ingredients must be dry before adding the vinaigrette, to insure even coating.
• Vinaigrettes can be used for dipping sauces, glazes, or marinades.
• A fast, simple method for making a vinaigrette is to place everything in a bottle and shake.

Here are three easy vinaigrettes showing the varying degree of special ingredients you can add to create a delicious dressing.

Oregano and Mustard Vinaigrette

⅓ cup red wine vinegar
½ teaspoon salt
1 teaspoon Dijon
  mustard
¼ teaspoon freshly
  ground pepper

1 garlic clove, minced
½ teaspoon dried
  oregano
⅔ cup extra virgin olive
  oil

1. In a bowl, add vinegar and salt. Whisk to blend.

2. Add mustard, pepper, garlic, and oregano. Continue whisking.

3. Slowly whisk in olive oil until thickened.

Pomegranate and Basil Vinaigrette

⅓ cup balsamic vinegar
½ teaspoon salt
1 tablespoon fresh basil,
  chopped
¼ teaspoon freshly
  ground pepper

1 shallot, minced
2 tablespoons
  pomegranate
  concentrate
⅔ cup extra virgin olive
  oil

1. In a bowl, add balsamic vinegar and salt. Whisk together.

2. Add basil, pepper, shallot and pomegranate concentrate. Whisk all ingredients together.

3. Slowly whisk in extra virgin olive oil until thickened.

NOTE: Pomegranate concentrate is pomegranate juice that has been reduced down to a syrup consistency, without adding sugar. It can be found in Middle Eastern markets or you can make your own: bring 2 cups of pomegranate juice to boil, then reduce the heat to low. Continue cooking until the liquid is reduced to ¼ cup, about 20 minutes.

Lavender Vinaigrette

⅓ cup sherry vinegar
½ teaspoon salt
1 teaspoon fresh lavender
  buds
1 teaspoon fresh thyme

1 teaspoon fresh
  marjoram
¼ teaspoon freshly
  ground pepper
1 shallot, minced
⅔ cup extra virgin olive oil

1. In a bowl, add vinegar and salt. Whisk together.

2. Add lavender, thyme, marjoram, pepper, and shallot. Whisk all ingredients together.

3. Slowly whisk in extra virgin olive oil until thickened.

The addition of olive oil produces a very smooth and creamy ice cream that you will never forget. Serve it alongside a nutty biscotti, roasted pears, or fresh berries. For even more exotic flavors, use lemon, blood orange, or jalapeño flavored olive oils.

Olive Oil and Vanilla Ice Cream

YIELD: 1½ QUARTS
PREP TIME: 10 MINUTES
COOK TIME: 15 MINUTES
CHILL TIME: 8 HOURS

1 cup granulated sugar
6 egg yolks
⅔ cup extra virgin olive oil
3 cups whole milk
1 cup heavy cream
2 teaspoons vanilla
1 teaspoon kosher salt

1. In a small nonstick pot over medium heat, whisk together with a hand mixer sugar and egg yolks until pale in color, about 5 minutes.

2. Add olive oil in a steady stream, and continue whisking until smooth and airy, about 3 minutes.

3. Add milk, cream, vanilla, and salt and whisk until combined.

4. Remove from heat, and allow mixture to cool to room temperature.

5. Transfer mixture into a bowl and cover. Refrigerate until chilled, about 2 hours.

6. Pour cream mixture into an ice cream maker, and freeze according to manufacturer's instructions.

7. Serve alone or with fresh fruit. Drizzle with fruit flavored olive oil of your choice.

Roasting with Olive Oil

There are many misconceptions about cooking with olive oil at high heat. The general consensus is that various factors affect the smoking point of an oil. The more refined an oil is, the lower the free fatty acids, thus producing a higher smoking point. But good quality extra virgin olive oils in their purest form are naturally low in free fatty acids. Therefore, they have a high smoking point and are safe for roasting.

Roasted Baby Carrots with Thyme

SERVES 4
PREP TIME: 5 MINUTES
COOK TIME: 25 MINUTES

16 baby carrots, trimmed
1 tablespoon extra virgin olive oil
¼ teaspoon salt
⅛ teaspoon freshly ground pepper
1 tablespoon fresh thyme

1. Preheat oven to 385°F.

2. Arrange carrots in one layer on a baking sheet.

3. Coat carrots with olive oil and season with salt and pepper.

4. Roast in oven until fork tender, about 25 minutes. Transfer carrots to a serving platter, garnish with fresh thyme, and serve.

Other great vegetables to roast are Brussels sprouts, potatoes, asparagus, and green beans.

A simple roast chicken is a staple on the family menu. This versatile meal is perfect alone, used for leftovers, or in countless other recipes. Fresh herbs and lemon keep this bird from being boring.

Roast Chicken with Olive Oil, Lemon, and Herbs

SERVES 4
PREP TIME: 15 MINUTES
COOK TIME: 1 HOUR, 20 MINUTES

3½ pound whole roasting chicken
2-3 tablespoons extra virgin olive oil
1 lemon, sliced
1 onion, quartered
1 sprig fresh mint
1 sprig fresh basil
2 sprigs fresh thyme
¼ teaspoon salt
⅛ teaspoon freshly ground pepper

1. About 30 minutes before roasting, remove chicken from the refrigerator. If the giblets and neck are in chicken cavity, remove them and reserve or discard.

2. Preheat oven to 425ºF.

3. Place chicken (breast side up) on a cast iron skillet or roasting pan, and rub entire chicken with olive oil. Season outside and cavity with salt and pepper.

4. Run your hands and olive oil underneath the skin of breast and thigh to loosen. Slide lemon slices under the skin.

5. Stuff remaining lemon slices, onion, and herbs into chicken cavity.

6. Using kitchen twine, tie chicken legs together and tuck wing tips under chicken.

7. Roast for 15 minutes, then lower oven temperature to 350ºF. Cook until a meat thermometer inserted into the thickest part of the thigh registers 170º-175ºF, approximately 1 to 1½ hours.

8. Remove from the oven, cover with foil, and let chicken stand for 10 minutes,

9. Serve in the skillet or transfer to a serving platter.

What can you drizzle with olive oil and eat raw? Just about anything. A delicious olive oil will enhance the flavor of any food or drink. Yes, drink! Olive oil can taste fruity, and a splash of it is all you need in this watermelon shooter. The three layers of flavor are poured in one at a time and naturally separate into their layers. Remember, the key to enjoying olive oil "in the raw" is to select an oil that has the right flavor and intensity that appeals to you.

Watermelon Shooters with Persian Mint Syrup and Olive Oil

SERVES 16 SHOTS

PERSIAN MINT SYRUP

1 cup granulated sugar
3½ cups water
¼ cup white wine vinegar
½ cup fresh mint, loosely packed

WATERMELON SHOOTER

3 pounds seedless watermelon, peeled and chopped
½ cup fresh orange juice
1 cup vodka (optional)
⅓ cup Persian mint syrup
8 teaspoons extra virgin olive oil, divided
zest from 1 orange, grated

1. To make the mint syrup, whisk water and sugar in a small pot over medium-high heat until dissolved.

2. Let syrup boil for 5 to 10 minutes, then add vinegar.

3. Reduce heat to medium, and cook until syrup thickens, about 20 to 30 minutes.

4. Remove from heat and stir in the fresh mint. Using a slotted spoon, remove mint when syrup has cooled.

5. To prepare your shooters, place the watermelon, orange juice, and vodka in a blender, and process until smooth.

6. Pour juice through a strainer to remove any seeds.

7. In a tall shot glass, add 1 teaspoon of cooled mint syrup.

8. Pour in 2 ounces of watermelon mix next.

9. Top with ½ teaspoon of olive oil and garnish with grated zest. Salut!

NOTE: This recipe will make ¾ cup of syrup, but you only need ⅓ cup of it to make 16 watermelon shooters. The syrup will keep in the refrigerator for up to one month. Dilute it with water to make a cooler or use as a dip with your romaine lettuce.

Cocktails go down smoothly with a little shot of olive oil. Choose an oil that suits your palate, but don't be afraid to try flavored oils like lemon, orange, or basil.

Finger Lime Kamikaze Shots with Mint and Olive Oil

SERVES 4 SHOTS

4 ounces vodka
2 ounces Triple Sec
2 ounces lemonade, homemade or store bought
2 teaspoons lemon infused extra virgin olive oil (½ teaspoon for each shot)
2 finger limes or key limes
½ teaspoon mint herb crystals (optional)
½ teaspoon fresh mint, minced

1. Shake until you have combined vodka, Triple Sec, and lemonade in a cocktail shaker full of ice.

2. Divide the drink into four shot glasses.

3. Top each shot glass with ½ teaspoon of olive oil.

4. Cut finger limes in half and gently massage and push out the round fruit inside. Top each shot glass with it. If you cannot find finger limes, squeeze half a key lime into each shot.

5. Top each shot with a few mint herb crystals or with sugar (optional).

6. Garnish with a bit of the minced fresh mint leaves.

NOTE: You can also serve lemonade without the alcohol and top with olive oil.

Conversion Charts

Baking Substitutions	
Butter	**Extra Virgin Olive Oil**
1 cup	¾ cup
¾ cup	½ cup + 1 tablespoon
⅔ cup	½ cup
½ cup	⅓ cup + 1 tablespoon
⅓ cup	¼ cup
¼ cup	3 tablespoons
⅛ cup	1½ tablespoons
1 tablespoon	4½ teaspoons
1 pound = 16 ounces = 454 grams	1½ cups
¾ pound = 12 ounces = 340 grams	1 cup
½ pound = 8 ounces = 227 grams	¾ cup
¼ pound = 4 ounce s= 113 grams	⅓ cup + 1 tablespoon
⅛ pound = 2 ounces = 57 grams	3 tablespoons

Temperature	
Degrees Fareneheit	Degrees Celsius
130°	54°
140°	60°
160°	71°
165°	74°
180°	82°
225°	107°
275°	135°
300°	149°
325°	163°
350°	177°
375°	191°
400°	204°
450°	232°

Kitchen Measurements

1 gallon = 4 quarts = 8 pints = 16 cups

½ gallon = 2 quarts = 4 pints = 8 cups

¼ gallon = 1 quart = 2 pints = 4 cups

⅛ gallon = ½ quart = 1 pint = 2 cups

½ quart = 1 pint = 2 cups = 16 fluid ounces

¼ quart = ½ pint = 1 cup = 8 fluid ounces

1 cup = 8 fluid ounces = 16 tablespoons = 48 teaspoons

¾ cup = 6 fluid ounces = 12 tablespoons = 36 teaspoons

⅔ cup = 5⅓ fluid ounces = 10 tablespoons = 32 teaspoons

½ cup = 4 fluid ounces = 8 tablespoons = 24 teaspoons

⅓ cup = 2⅔ fluid ounces = 5 tablespoons = 16 teaspoons

¼ cup = 2 fluid ounces = 4 tablespoons = 12 teaspoons

⅛ cup = 1 fluid ounce = 2 tablespoons = 6 teaspoons

½ fluid ounces = 1 tablespoon = 3 teaspoons

SOURCES
Culinary Institute, *Healthy Cooking* (Wiley, 2008)
Culinary Institute, *Vegetarinan Cooking* (Wiley, 2008)
Dornenburg, Andrew, *Culinary Artistry* (Wiley, 1996)
Escoffier, Auguste, *The Escoffier* (Potter, 1969)
Herbst, Sharon, *Food Lover's Companion* (Barron's, 2007)
McGee, Harold, *On Food and Cooking* (Scribner, 2004)
Mueller, Tom, *Extra Virginity* (W.W.Norton, 2012)
Page, Karen and Andrew Dornenberg, *The Flavor Bible* (Little Brown, 2008)
Pepin, Jacques, *Complete Techniques* (Black Dog, 2001)

WEBSITE ARTICLES
Cater, Nancy, "San Diego Olives: Origins of a California Industry,"
    sandiegohistory.org
Flynn, Dr. Mary, Boston University, "How Eating Can Save Your Life," bu.edu
Mayo Clinic, "Mediterranean Diet," mayoclinic.com
Oldways, "Mediterranean Diet," oldwayspt.org
U.C. Davis Olive Oil Website, "Evaluation of Extra Virgin Olive Oil,"
    olivecenter.ucdavis.edu

ONLINE SOURCES
Australian Olive Association, australianolives.com.au
California Olive Oil Council, cooc.com
California State University at Sonoma,
    cesonoma.ucanr.edu
International Olive Council, internationaloliveoil.org
North American Olive Oil Association, naooa.org
Olive Oil Times, oliveoiltimes.com
Olive Oil Source, oliveoilsource.com
The Olive Press, theolivepress.com
U.C. Davis Olive Center, olivecenter.ucdavis.edu

TWO EXTRA VIRGINS ONLINE SITES
Two Extra Virgins, twoextravirgins.com
Everything Olive Oil , Google Plus,
    plus.google.com communities/108062450450070454160
Everything Olive Oil, Pinterest,
    pinterest.com/califgreekgirl/everything-olive-oil
Two Extra Virgins, Facebook, facebook.com/TwoExtraVirgins

Recipe Index

Are
you
ready to

imagine
"olive"
the
possibilities?